I Am a GYMNAST

As photographed
by Jane Feldman

Random House 🏠 New York

To Lena, Kalina, Ayannah, Chamisa, Kelsey, Sarah, Tyson, Jannelle, Grayson, Phoebe, Ali, James Patrick, Michaelangelo, Emily, Alex, Katya, and McKenzie—the youngest dreamers of my extended family. They are my most constructive critics and surround me with constant inspiration. To all those who strive to be the best they can be, both as individuals and as team players. And, of course, to the dreamer in all of us!

All rights reserved under International and Pan-American Copyright Conventions. Published in the United States by Random House, Inc., New York, and simultaneously in Canada by Random House of Canada Limited, Toronto. Distributed by Random House, Inc., New York.
All photographs, including front and back cover, copyright © 2000 by Jane Feldman, with the exception of the photograph on page 20 © 1998 by Kristine Larsen for Essence Communications.

www.randomhouse.com/kids

Library of Congress Cataloging-in-Publication Data
Feldman, Jane. I am a gymnast / as photographed by Jane Feldman. p. cm. — (Young dreamers)
SUMMARY: Seven-year-old McKenzie Foster describes her training, practice, and performance as a rhythmic gymnast.
ISBN 0-375-80251-7 (trade) — ISBN 0-375-90251-1 (lib. bdg.)
1. Foster, McKenzie—Juvenile literature. 2. Foster, McKenzie—Pictorial works—Juvenile literature. 3. Gymnasts—United States—Biography—Juvenile literature.
[1. Foster, McKenzie. 2. Gymnasts.] I. Title. II. Series.
GV460.2.F68 F45 2000 796.44'092—dc21 [B] 00-026216
Printed in the United States of America June 2000 10 9 8 7 6 5 4 3 2 1
RANDOM HOUSE and colophon are registered trademarks of Random House, Inc.

There are five people in my family: Mommy; Daddy;
my sister, Drew; my brother, Jack; and me. We kids are all
one and a half years apart. I'm the littlest. We live in a town called
Riverdale, which is part of New York City.

Drew and I share a bedroom. That's okay because we get along great.
It's nice having a best friend to talk to all the time.

Hi! You don't know me yet,
but maybe someday you will.
I'm McKenzie Foster, and I'm almost eight.
My favorite thing in the world
is gymnastics.

$\mathcal{T}$his book came to be as a huge "team effort." First of all, I would like to thank McKenzie for her enthusiasm and her wonderful family—the Fosters. I would also like to thank Wendy Hilliard for her extraordinary efforts not only in helping to make this book happen but also in her continued work with young people. I would also like to thank Wendy's family for their undying support of her over the years, and also her coach, Dr. Zina Mironov, who not only introduced her to rhythmic gymnastics but also gave her extraordinary training, both as a gymnast and as a coach.

I would like to acknowledge the board members, staff, volunteers, parents, contributors, sponsors, and friends of the Wendy Hilliard Foundation and Rhythmic Gymnastics NY as well as Armory High School Sports Foundation; USA Gymnastics, especially Steve Penny, for coordinating National Gymnastics Day/NY; *The Today Show,* for hosting National Gymnastics Day; NYC 2012; Sutton Gymnastics; Isadora/Big Apple Rhythmics; ANTI-GRAVITY; Flip City; Forest Hills Rhythmics; the folks at Capezio 57th St., NYC; and the Ballet Company, NYC.

A special thank-you to all the girls on the RGNY team, who are all stars in their own right!

I would like to extend my gratitude to our very special athletes who supported this book, but who also inspire us all—Bela Karolyi, Shannon Miller, Dominique Dawes, Tatyana Brikulskaya, and Ryan Weston.

To the amazing staff at Random House—especially Kate Klimo, Georgia Morrissey, Susan Lovelace, and Kenneth LaFreniere—for their constant support and encouragement in this and the other books in the Young Dreamers series.

To Chelsea Black & White Custom Lab and to the folks at Westside Color. To the staff of Fotocare for their constant T.L.C.

To my CityKids and Darrow School families.

To my nuclear and extended family—with special thanks to my mothers, Dawn and Birdie; to my father and Myra; to my sister Jill and her family; to Bill and Maria and their family; and to a very special friend who has always been there for me, and who introduced me to Wendy Hilliard originally, Joanne Golden.

To Erika Stone and Lari Brandstein (both mentors through the years), to Melvin Estrella, and to the one and only Michelle McHugh.

And to the Creator—the source of all creativity.

All three of us go to the same school. We walk home together afterward and try to get our homework done before Mommy and Daddy get home.

One of the things I like best about gymnastics is I can do it anywhere. I can do it on the lawn in front of my apartment building.

My sister thinks I look like Gumby when I stretch in this green bodysuit.

$\mathcal{I}$ can also do gymnastics on the beach.

Being at the beach
gives me a sense of
freedom, but it is hard
to work on the sand.

$\mathcal{B}$ut the best place to do gymnastics is in the gym!

There are six types of gymnastics: artistic, rhythmic, trampoline, tumbling, sport acrobatics, and sport aerobics. When I was four, I started doing artistic gymnastics. That's the kind where you get to use the balance beam, the uneven bars, the vault, and the floor.

Only boys compete on the rings because it requires great upper-body strength. But I thought I'd give it a try.

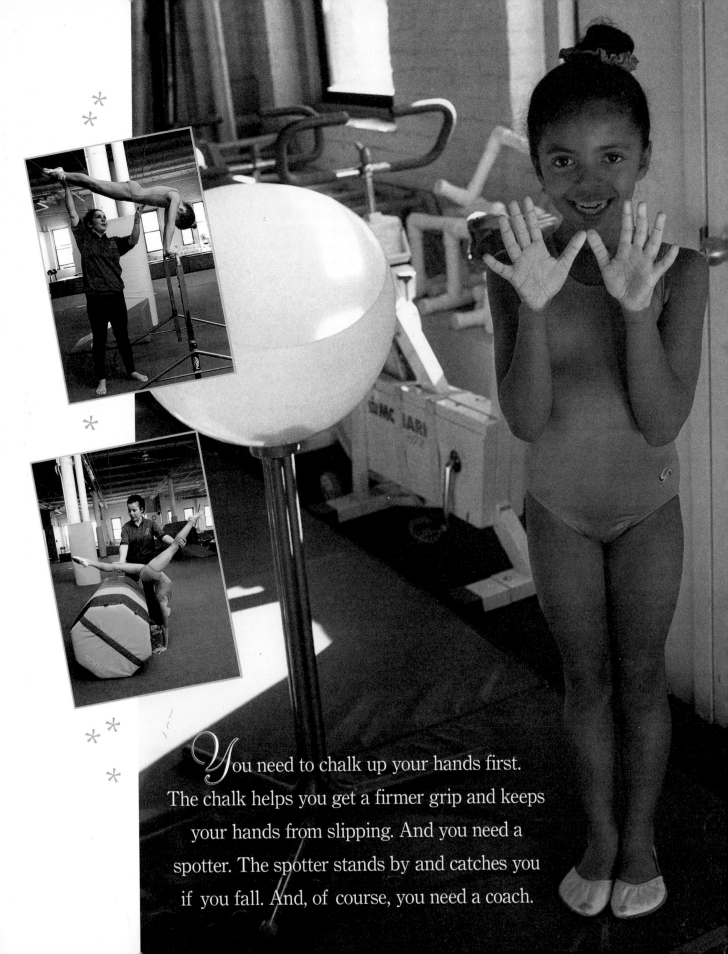

ou need to chalk up your hands first. The chalk helps you get a firmer grip and keeps your hands from slipping. And you need a spotter. The spotter stands by and catches you if you fall. And, of course, you need a coach.

When I was six, my artistic coach, Veronica, introduced me to Wendy Hilliard, who became my rhythmic coach, and now I work with both of them. They thought I'd be a natural at rhythmic gymnastics.

The difference between rhythmic and artistic gymnastics is that in artistic, you work *on* an apparatus—like the balance beam or the uneven bars—and in rhythmic, you must work *with* an apparatus—like the rope, the hoop, the ball, or the ribbon.

*R*hythmic
gymnastics
is a combination
of athleticism
and awesome
coordination.

What makes rhythmic gymnastics fun is that the routines are choreographed, just like in dance. You have to remember all the steps, control your equipment, and keep moving to the beat of the music—all at the same time!

You compete either as an individual or on a team. On a team, you all have to do the moves at the same time—*and* make them look easy! This is my team.

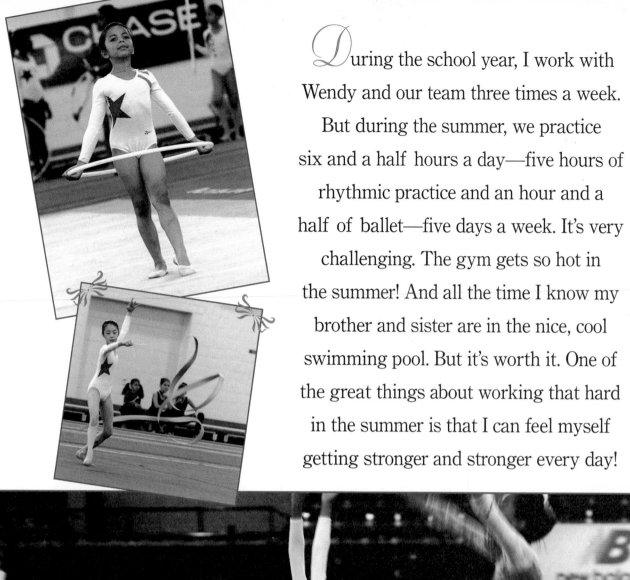

During the school year, I work with Wendy and our team three times a week. But during the summer, we practice six and a half hours a day—five hours of rhythmic practice and an hour and a half of ballet—five days a week. It's very challenging. The gym gets so hot in the summer! And all the time I know my brother and sister are in the nice, cool swimming pool. But it's worth it. One of the great things about working that hard in the summer is that I can feel myself getting stronger and stronger every day!

Wendy is an amazing coach. She works us very hard, but we know she loves us and wants what's best for us. She demands the best from us every single day, even though some days I come in and I'm tired and I'd rather not be there. Wendy works us hard because she has always worked hard herself.

As a matter of fact, Wendy was the first African-American woman ever to compete in rhythmic gymnastics for the United States gymnastics team. She traveled for ten years, to over fifteen countries, and won lots of medals. Wendy even trained an Olympian! The girls on my team come from all different backgrounds, and that's because Wendy worked so hard to pave the way for the rest of us.

Veronica is still a part of my life, too. She works with Wendy and the team several days a week. It's important to Wendy to give an opportunity to kids who wouldn't otherwise get a chance to study gymnastics, so she created the Wendy Hilliard Foundation, which provides gymnastics classes for kids. She works hard with us, both as individuals and as a team. Getting us to work as a team is part of her daily challenge. Wendy would love it if we all went on to compete in the Olympics, but what really counts to her is that we all learn to respect our bodies, work together as a team, become strong, and stretch our bodies as well as our minds!

$\mathscr{B}$efore we begin class,
Wendy has us do plenty of stretching
to warm up our muscles. If you don't stretch,
you could pull a muscle—
and that *really* hurts!

$\mathcal{P}$eople sometimes ask me
if it's hard to do splits.
Well, it takes a lot
of practice—and *lots*
of stretching.

After practicing so hard, the exciting thing is when we get to compete. Competitions are held all over the country, but we compete in the New York City area. Wendy's working hard to bring the Olympics to New York City in 2012. Wouldn't that be amazing?

This meet is called the New York City Championships. Girls of all ages and sizes come—the littlest ones are four years old, like me when I started. (At four you can perform, and at six you can start competing.) The girls' mothers come with them and do their hair, and of course Mommy does mine. Just like dancers, we need to keep our hair out of our faces because the judges want to see our neck muscles.

The competitions, which are usually held in big gymnasiums, always start off with a procession of all the teams— just like in the Olympics! Because I'm the smallest, I get to lead my team into the gym. It's okay that I'm little. I'm used to it. I'm the littlest at home and the littlest on the team. It just makes me work that much harder! I get nervous sometimes, but I'm always very proud! The sign I'm carrying says RGNY, which stands for Rhythmic Gymnastics New York. That's my team!

Just like in practice, we warm up before we compete. Each coach gives her team a little pep talk to get them psyched for the competition. Some of these teams have traveled a long way to get here. It's great to meet gymnasts from other places.

We wear half-shoes, which help us turn and point our feet.

Our team costume is red, white, and blue. The bigger girls get to wear purple. That's my favorite color.

Performance routines are a special part of the meet.
Some teams wear very theatrical costumes—and even sunglasses!

I love playing dress-up
at home. I can't wait to do it
in performance.

There are so many incredibly wonderful performances at the meet.
I sure wouldn't want to be the judge.

After everybody has competed, we sit quietly
in our team formations and wait while the judges
make their decision. We all feel a little nervous
and *a lot* excited.

When the judges call us to the podium as a team,
it feels like we all win!

This year, Wendy and the whole team are invited, along with some of the greatest gymnasts in the country, to help celebrate National Gymnastics Day. Some of these gymnasts are even going to be competing in the 2000 Olympics in

Sydney. Wendy takes us to Rockefeller Center. We get up very early because *The Today Show* is filming us for TV and we have to be there at five o'clock in the morning! It is very hard dragging ourselves out of bed that early, but when we get there, it is worth it.

We get to see some of my favorite gymnasts. We see Ryan Weston doing a demonstration on the trampoline, which is one of my favorite parts of gymnastics. He bounces higher than four stories! People are staring out the windows. They can't believe it! This year, for the first time, trampoline is being offered at the Olympics.

This is Brenda Jones with Ryan and Wendy. Brenda makes sure all of Wendy's RGNY classes run smoothly.

$\mathcal{I}$t is so exciting. We meet gold medalists Nadia Comaneci and Kerri Strug. It is amazing to meet them in person. I have always watched them in the Olympics on TV. The whole team gets to pose for photographers and news cameras with Shannon Miller and Dominique Dawes and Olympic coach Bela Karolyi. That's Veronica on Bela's right. They knew each other in Romania. Bela coached some of the greatest gymnastics stars ever, like Nadia Comaneci, Mary Lou Retton, and Kerri Strug. He comes and talks to me and encourages me to keep up the good work!

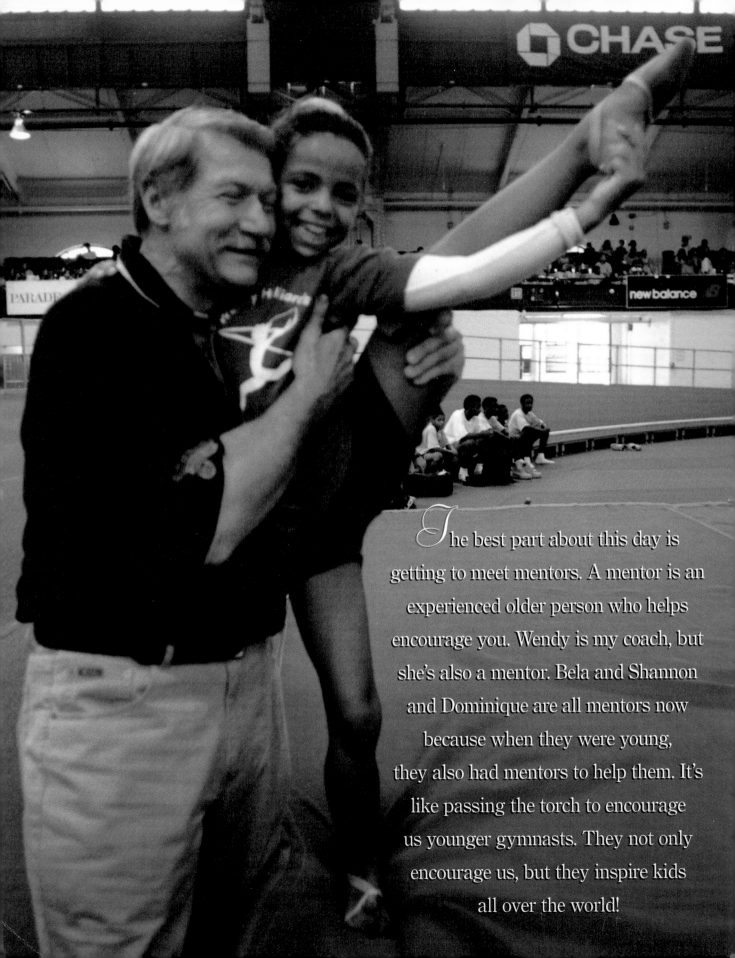

The best part about this day is getting to meet mentors. A mentor is an experienced older person who helps encourage you. Wendy is my coach, but she's also a mentor. Bela and Shannon and Dominique are all mentors now because when they were young, they also had mentors to help them. It's like passing the torch to encourage us younger gymnasts. They not only encourage us, but they inspire kids all over the world!

In the afternoon, we go to the gym. It's inside this big building called the Armory Track & Field Center. Our team, along with other teams, gets to perform for Bela and Shannon.

Afterward, they give us lots of encouragement. They sound just like Wendy. They say it's not *all* about going to the Olympics. It's about working hard, believing in yourself, and being the best you that you can possibly be!

With Bela and Shannon and Dominique in the
audience this day, we all give it our very best!

$\mathcal{T}$his is Tatyana. She is one of the best rhythmic gymnasts in the whole country and has won lots of medals. She used to be on my RGNY team, but Wendy suggested she should train with her friend Nataliya because Tatyana needs to practice five to six days a week to be so great. When she is not competing, she is a star performer with the ANTI-GRAVITY gymnastics company in New York City.

🌀

$\mathcal{S}$utton's Team had these
great robot guys. They
sure were strong! This is
Sasha. He competed
in artistic gymnastics
for Russia.

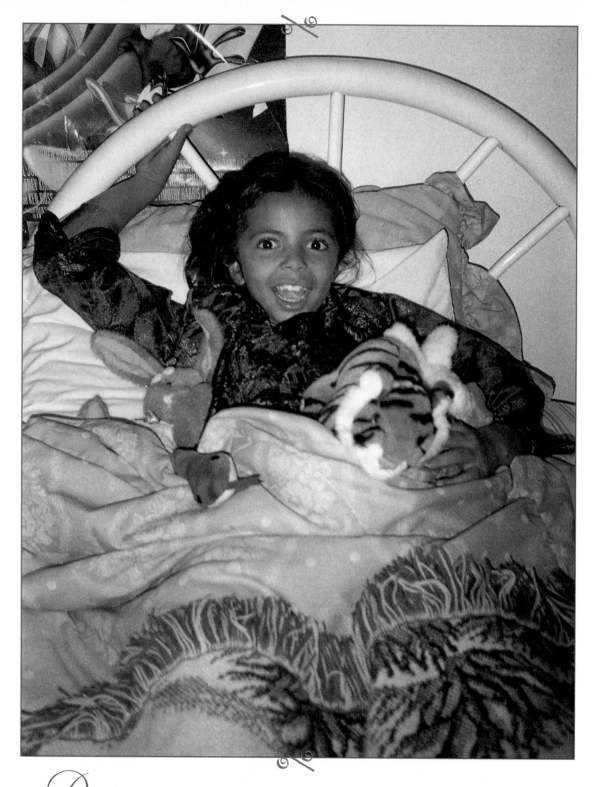

After the most exciting day of my life, I should be exhausted,
since I've been up since four o'clock in the morning,
but I just keep thinking about what an amazing day it has been.

The only thing I imagine could be more exciting would be standing on the Olympic podium someday and receiving the gold medal!

Jane Feldman is a professional photographer whose striking work has gained international attention in the field of advertising and among nonprofit organizations that promote youth empowerment. This is Ms. Feldman's third book in her Young Dreamers series, which also includes *I Am a Dancer* and *I Am a Rider*. A native New Yorker, Ms. Feldman divides her time between Manhattan and the Berkshire Mountains in Massachusetts.